Canst thou draw out leviathan with an hook?

About the author

Roger Finch was born in Pittsburgh in 1937, studied music theory at George Washington University, and subsequently received a doctorate in Near Eastern Languages and Literatures from Harvard. Since the late 1970s he has lived in Japan, teaching at Sophia University in Tokyo and currently as Professor at Surugadai University, Saitama. His wide experience of Asia, as scholar and traveller, is reflected in his poetry, as is also his engagement with other cultures and with questions of family, social and sexual identity. He has published in poetry journals, in chapbooks, and in one previous highly-praised full collection, *According to Lilies* (1992).

By the same author

According to Lilies (Carcanet, 1992)

FOX IN THE
MORNING

ROGER FINCH

LEVIATHAN
OXFORD · PORTLAND · AMSTERDAM

First published in Great Britain in 2000 by
Leviathan
Market House
Market Place
Deddington
Oxford OX15 0SE

© Roger Finch, 2000

Roger Finch is hereby identified as the author of this work
in accordance with the Copyright, Designs and Patents Act 1988

A CIP record for this book is available from the British Library

ISBN 1-903563-05-4 (cased)
1-903563-06-2 (paperback)

Editorial Director
Michael Hulse

Editorial Advisers
John Kinsella, Anne Michaels, Vincent O'Sullivan

Design
Claire Brodmann

Typesetting
Jeff Hames

Sales and Marketing
Drake International Services, Deddington, Oxford OX15 0SE

Distribution
BDL, Learoyd Road, Mountfield Industrial Estate, New Romney TN28 8XU

Printing and Binding
T. J. International Ltd., Padstow, Cornwall PL28 8RW

Contents

*This book is
dedicated to
Louis M. Hargan*

Acknowledgements

Certain of the poems that appear in this collection have previously been published by *The Beloit Poetry Journal*, *The Cape Rock*, *Cimarron Review*, *Descant*, *Envoi*, *Kansas Quarterly*, *The Literary Review*, *Mississippi Valley Review*, *Orbis*, *Poet Lore*, *San Jose Studies*, *Stand* and *The Wormwood Review*.

Listening to Bells on New Year's Eve

The child, lifted in his grandfather's arms, first feels
    the bronze honey from the bells
  on the drumheads of the soles of his feet.
   Their violet veins, as delicate
as the network on the skins of crocus bulbs,
throb and throb, only milliseconds behind
the bark of his heart. His whole body is wet

with the thick dark sound. Its spell has transformed him
    into an early Baroque
  gilt-bronze cupid. He glows in the mild
  citron-colored halo from bridge lamps.
His mother looks up at him. Her arms swan's-neck
from petunia-shaped black-and-white chiffon sleeves,
and on the pillar of her throat, where the gold

chain would be a garland of carved wooden roses
    if her throat were the pillar
  of a harp, her young husband's kiss shows
  as clearly as a panther's rosette.
The child sees his mother's face draped with a mask
where the lamp's shade starts, but the lower half flares
with the richness of bells as his mouth plucks hers.

"I Never Saw a Saw . . ."

I never saw a saw like this saw saws
my father drones in my ear as he lifts me
into the bath. For some reason, my eyes fix
     on the white enamel gas heater
     on the shelf above the tub, the flame
inside making devil's eyes through the goat's-eyed
slots. I associate the snake sounds Father makes

     with the looks the stove is giving me
and for years I will have nightmares about it.
I sob slightly as I sit in the blood-warm
     water. Father undresses and slides in
     too, restfully hugging me. His gun
floats softly and pinkly against me. I try
to squirt it as I squirt my own pudgy worm

     and Father makes it stand up and bark
at me. *I never saw a saw like this saw saws*
he says again as he pulls the plug and bluffs
     me with the evil maelstrom that empties
     down the drain. This time I scream and bawl.
Father's incantation has the power to raise
demons. I kick at him. Father only laughs

     and presses me ever more tightly
against his naked body. I feel the eel-smooth
skin slither along me, as slippery as sperm,
     and from the mud of my fright, one hot
     stem of infant sexuality swarms
spineward, opening its thousand fragrant petals
in me as I lie blissfully on his arm.

Dancing in the Churchill Lounge

To the two-year-old boy in Booth 5,
    the dancers are a garden, slow blooms
beneath showlight, his mother in her red crepe dress
    a hollyhock amidst lighter flowers.
    He stands on the seat to gaze at them,
the satiny turn, turn, and his hair has the gilt
from white, yellow, red in strings above his head.
    And then they are back and he is caught
in red swirls, his mother's breath raspberry sweet
    on his mouth, and cool, from the tall cool pink
    she is sipping. His smile is her smile.
Photographs from those years show them with same cheeks,
    same lips, same eyes. At fourteen, the fit

    is even closer. That Hallowe'en
    I put on the red crepe dress, wore a wig,
reddened my mouth. My mirror showed me, in the realm
    inside the frame, the portrait of one
    from an evening that I only then
remembered. Jewelry was superfluous. On the skin
of the boy I was just outgrowing bloomed
    the beauty of the one I loved the best.
Father was disturbed, but he danced with me, waltzed
    me across beneath the orange-and-black
    of let's pretend. I felt his breath on my ear.
And smiled. Still Mother's smile, but with a hint of my own smile,
    the smile of one far too often kissed.

The Iron Deer

Victorian signature, practices
its dainty quadruped *en pointe* on a lawn
          swept with peacocks. East Park, just across
          the railroad bridge to Grandmother's house,
had one, forever stalagmatized to its place
          beside the pond. We admired the gloss

of its flanks, contracted from the fine
sebaceous oils of the Nordic-white shanks
          of the children who mounted it; the prance
          its feet seemed to make as we rode it;
its ten-tined rack that carded the summer clouds.
          I have a photograph that one glance

will show is Very Near Utopia:
me on the deer and, beside me, Grandfather
          in his summer whites, the only match
          we had for summer clouds; Grandmother
on the other side is an upright pansy bed
          (though this is black & white) with a patch

of verbenas garlanding her head.
Poor Grandpa! Poor Grandma! They were forced to move
          when The Blacks arrived, for everyone
          knows that Blacks will systematically
denigrate the property values, and all
          of their Utopias were undone,

part of the faded past. I was afraid
of this: the deer signed "Zeke" in dayglo orange,
          or, worse still, hammered, gutted and gored.
          But The Blacks have gone, the rents have soared,
and the deer still stands, stands still, without human
          patina but otherwise restored.

Hunting Macaws

(A drawing by Riou, based on J. Crevaux)
Voyage dans l'Amérique du Sud, Paris, 1883

Open the book and there! (triumphant)
    it is. Isn't it the same? The same:
the one just after the Elephant

with Howdah (housing Rajah & Sons)
    just after Malabar Pepper Trees
just after Fiji Grass Huts (the name

C. – or is it G.? – Riou coiled
    in the lower left corner). If you
riffle my mind you'll find them with ease,

listed so: those detailed engravings
    that, in days before photography,
provided the only peekaboo

our grandparents knew of the wide, wide,
    curious, and wonderful world outside
their own. I still recall that heavy

tome of Grandmother's, brought all the way
    from England, with its moiré paper
binding and four triangular hide

corners – shaped liked the Photocorners
    we used to mount pictures in albums –
their edges worn to dust. Then there were

the pages themselves, tan-ivory,
    mackled with old-age freckles like buds
of rust. At the leafing of my thumbs

5

the entire world flipped beneath my eyes.
　　　　Turn to p. 90, "Hunting Macaws":
there we see (or barely see, due to floods

of ink meant to represent shadows)
　　　　a hunter kneeling in the lower
boughs of a tree, the self bow he draws

half-veiled beneath what appears to be
　　　　a thatch of dry grass, ostensibly
a hunter's-blind. Against the long fur

of the sky, a few macaws are seen
　　　　silhouetted: two of them are clipped
conveniently to a bare branch; three

or four more emerge from a threadbare
　　　　patch where the sun is presumed to shine,
rendered in that shorthand sort of script

artists use for "birds in flight": limp v's
　　　　drooping in the heat. The text introduced
a Tembé myth: "Once upon a time,

there were two brothers. One made himself
　　　　a hide-out in an azywaywa tree,
the flowers of which the macaws used

to come and eat. He had already
　　　　killed numbers of birds, when two jaguars
appeared on the scene carrying many

gourds which they filled with sweet nectar pressed
        from the blossoms of the tree . . ." The myth
then recounts how one of the brothers

was killed and how the other went off
        to the anthill where the jaguars dwelt
and found honey. What we're concerned with

here is not the story itself (quaint
        thought it may be) or "the origin
of the honey festival" (it is felt

that the story explains this) but what
        the tokens mean that are stashed behind.
The macaws, of course, are the lightnings

of recall that strike the hollow bole
        where the honey is stored; the jaguars
of remembrance circle beneath the blind,

expressing flowers; honey, with its rind
        of wax, is joy past; the honey-feast
is poetry, festival of the mind.

Mother and I at South Park

She stands behind me, her hands
on my shoulders. My small face
is a smaller denomination of hers,
sovereign's prince. Our English silver gleams
in the best American sunlight, the wheels
of Bicycles for Rent behind us,
cut from the centers of hundreds of India's flags,
greater but lesser coins struck in the same mint.
Our smiles unsteel the onlooker. Back then
it was the old man who ran the shop
(we see him on the left-hand side),
so charmed he lifted his parrot from its stand
to show me, its long greens splashing down in paint

from a mix of yellows and blues.
At Rheims we see an angel smile
that way, the sitter's uncorrupted grace still clear
in the corrupted stone. I can live,
from this brief impression of us, one whole day
with her, turn and lay my head against her,
recapture the smell of clean cotton from her dress.
The boys's smile, no. Time smudges even pearl. His gold
in its undersea takes on the same lime
that makes pearl, in weird wormings and crusts.
We see, in the photograph
with Father, tantrum held down by Father's hand,
beneath the shine the temper of a ghost child.

What Is Written on the Back of a Photograph

Wilber and Marlyn
Riverview Park, 1947

Pretty boy. An angel. His grandfather's hat
    is a halo around his head, his smile
    painted by brush by Fra Angelico.
    We did not know that day was next to,
no, nearest perfect, bright star in that long night sky
    that is childhood, pretty little girl,
        his sister, on the boy's lap,
the Madonna behind but out of the view finder,
all smiles by Fra Angelico. And then I spot,
in the lower right-hand corner, a small blonde head.
    That is the Other Sister, "asleep"
on the Indian blanket, its red-purple, green,
and white suddenly fixed by magic-lantern light,

the feel of the wool beneath my hand the feel
    of 1947: sun, locks of grass,
    dead-ripe honeydew, the feather weight
    of Grandfather's white straw hat. It lives
even in the Other Sister's barrette, quite plain
    in the photograph, its color – pink – won
        by memory from black-and-white.
We wonder why the Other Sister did not face
the camera. Odd blonde out of five, the rest of them
brunette, she sulked when we smiled, smirked when we were sad.
    On the back, in Aunt Marion's shaky hand:
Wilber and Marlyn. Fond of the girls, their doter
and dresser, here she did not write the other's name.

Patterns in Sunlight

(at Grandmother's farmhouse, 6 miles north of Butler, Pa.)

1

Sunlight swells through the cambric curtains
with such force it swamps in gold
the surface of the dining table.
Pieces of my picture puzzle float in its tank,
too dazzling to touch;
its oranges and blues are washed several shades
lighter in it, making the fragments hard to match.

One wall is shaded, richly shaded
by the lilac's cordate leaves,
dark beacon for blazed eyes. It's the end
of the puzzle; it grew too fast, Cinderella's
mouse-drawn pumpkin coach.
This is the heart of the house. Here Grandma irons,
as she does now, or sews, or knits, as I sketch,

when the afternoon soap operas come on,
Ma Perkins, Stella Dallas,
and *Portia Faces Life.* I listen.
I solemnly listen. And the while she talks,
a chain of asides
that soon has us both crying with laughter under
Tragedy's wings like a pair of Shakespeare bawds.

2

The sun flows over the heart-shaped back
of the Victorian settee;
it melts the purple from the velvet's old rose,

making it almost the color of peachskin.
  A shawl of it drapes across my shoulder,
stamps its foil on the plum-black cover of my book.
Grandma suggested I read. I sit alone

    in the clock-quick, silk-darkened parlor.
      The front door is open to sieve
the August breeze, and from the porch the faint clink
of wind chimes, as though from a perpetual toast
      with delicate old wine glasses, mixes
with the whirring of wasps that live beneath the eaves.
Several zigzag twigs of morning glory twist

    over the book and under redgold letters:
      Mrs. A. D. T. Witney's
Stories. The title of this one is *We Girls.*
The pen-and-ink drawings might be of this house,
      the vine-wound railings, the old-fashioned
kitchen with its "deep iron sink". I read their speech
with a sense of belonging, my own lines to rehearse.

  3

    Sheets of sunshine flutter to the floor,
      telling leafgold how to cling
to the edges of chinaware, to the rims
      of all the glasses. Copper is plated
with it, silver is more precious, even pewter
has been rinsed with it and now is lusterware.
I have been lured from my book by the juice that foams

11

on the stove, sending out its winey scent
 throughout the house. Elderberry
jelly! The crushed pulp bleeds through from a gauze purse,
 giving to the golden vats below
its murex, a true royal purple, enough
to suffuse several robes of empire, to stain
the fine Syrian silk for an empress's dress.

4

Sunset shears through the mirror-backed leaves
 and polished chrysoprase fruit
 that canopy the grape arbor.
Such natural baroque grace may be observed
 on the border of a Sheffield plate
wine coaster or a pair of particularly fine
crewel-worked bed hangings. The sun fans now. Each pleat

 is as fine as the blade of a lance
 and each blade pierces a leaf.
 There are wires of it so sharp
one can needle a single grape without disturbing
 the one next to it. The grapes are green
now, greeny white, honeysuckle white, softly
bruising blue. Within a few weeks, the entire span

 will be wine-drizzling purple, frost-marked,
 busy with gnats. I have found
 an old chord zither in the attic
and have brought it here to play on as the sun
 drops. I hold it like a lyre, the warp
up and down, and play at Apollo. My fingers
are small childish winds on an Aeolian harp.

Nigger Lover

We called him "Fox". Our classmates
said we would be friends. He took dinner
at our house (when Father was away),
studied in my room, even stayed overnight
(when Father worked night
shift), slept beside me in the same bed.
I filled my memory's treasury with the sight

of his face across the desk
from me, filled sketchbooks with his body,
nude, filled my priest's bed with his vibrant
real or phantom presence. The place where he lay,
his skin intently
touching mine, grew small gold butterflies.
I gathered them up into the passageway

of my hands, closing goblet
fingers around their loosening wings.
It was his mouth that lived in that dark
chalice. How many times I secretly sipped
his passion from it!
I carried it with me as safely
as though his own heart fluttered there. My crushed script

begged him in notes to meet me
in night's confessional, near the lilacs
at the end of our yard. My footsteps
drew him toward me. He was teak against much
darker shadows. He
would smile, we'd embrace, our lips not
yet that close, though eventually they would touch.

The Man Who Is Shot from Guns

To the boy in the red-and-gray reindeer sweater
in the twelfth row, Harry the Human Cannonball
       is a comet made of silk,
      its oriflammes fluttering wildly
       around the wadded core as the man,
now fire, somersaults over and over in the air
at twice the speed of sound. He really is a star,

a shooting star, sudden as a meteor shower
that sinks the earth, as though the planetary floor
       were rushing headlong up, up
       toward the dome, and he really is fabric,
      for his cape barks like flags in high wind
as it tops his own trajectory. The smoke clears
and out of the steely maw a red fox soars,

brush waving. An act of daring that took hours
to perfect is over in seconds. No one suspects
       his tendons are wound wire-tight
      from his ankles to his neck, no one
      knows that, as he flies, his chest expands,
as though his muscles were wings, no one sees the fright
or joy in his face as he hurtles toward the net.

To the Lakeshore

A bird I hold in my hands,
    a bird beaded in turquoise,
his wings and tail and crest quilled with black and white.
Uneasily he beats, as a hand-held heart
    beats, but the bird's heart beats twice as fast,
two eighth-notes for every quarter-note of mine.
My fingers feel this clockwork, though it is soft-voiced

    beneath his robe; they also feel
    the pulse of his would-fly wings
lift in time with the lift of his breath against
the cage I am making with my hands. His eyes
    drill me; quietly they countermand
my sentence. There were seven of them, kingfishers,
fledglings; one by one I threw them to the wind

    and watched as their fans unlocked
    stiffly and brusquely in the first rush
of updraft their feathers ever felt. I raise
this one, the last, and slowly unfasten my clutch.
    He tests the emptiness and then breaks off
in a gust and clears the trees; he aims for the lake
but only makes the shore. That is far enough.

"All These Phenomena Are Important"

An ordinary dog
   on an ordinary country road
      one afternoon in August
is merely one of them. His progress along the shoulder
         of the road
is much the way an amateur pianist
interprets Chopin: long runs of the utmost

agitation, when
   the click of the dog's claws on asphalt
      may be correctly compared
to the sound of the pianist's fingernails
         as they assault
the white keys, interspersed with slack *rubato*
passages that represent those unexplored

stands of Wedgwood-blue
   chicory along the side of the road
      being examined by the dog
for signs of field mice, voles, thrashers, possibly
         a horned toad.
In one yard, an old truck tire has been whitewashed
and filled with Razzle Dazzle petunias. This was in vogue

forty years ago.
   To the curly-haired young man on the red
      Gitane, it seems that the dog
has stopped to smell the petunias. The dog will
         turn his head
and will try to make the sign that we call "smile",
as dogs always do when they greet us or beg

for something; the young man
    will not acknowledge the dog's affection,
       he will note only the bad taste
of petunias in a tire; he does not know
            anyone
like the elderly woman who planted them there.
The young man pedals on, spreading pinwheels of dust

where there might have been
    intelligent gossip shared for dry
       sherry in a professor's rooms
scattered with Japanese prints, if he had stopped.
          Soon the sky
will soak up that lint-sized spot that is a man
seated on a bicycle. It will take ten times

longer for the dog
    to disappear and the reader may stalk
       the ordinary dog-paced plan
of the poem as it heads purposefully
         at a walk
westward down the road, its tail held high, jaunty,
a little vulgar, until finally it is gone.

Proust Visits the Jeu de Paume

The note to Vaudoyer went out.
Perfect company. Just after nine
in the morning, his time to sleep, but today,
at the Jeu de Paume, he will see the Vermeers
all Paris is talking about. Black,
black & gray & white, his habit is complete.
In the hallway, the smell of raisins
in boiled milk. Sickly sweet,
the vapor turns on him as he rounds the stairs.

As wound as snail shell, as wound
as the cochlea inside the ear,
the steps spring up, ready to strike. The hair cells
inside his inner ear frazzle and he faints,
or nearly faints, reels, and rambles back.
Later, he will write that Bergotte dies in sight
of the *View of Delft*, lured from his bed
by a critic's praise, "precious piece
of Chinese art," victim of grandiloquence

and uremia. A bout
of dizziness, yes, and a "violent"
headache, but not the azotemic odor of the breath;
Proust is not uremic. He staggers on the path
as though drunk, still dazed from his attack,
but Vaudoyer will take his elbow, lead him
to "the loveliest picture in the world"
(which he has seen before). His one wish
now is that the last great moment will be death.

On the Nature of Angels

You have accurately noted how they tread
the airy waters of our upper-story
windows, summoning us to an exalted
final swim, and you have noted how they fall
into the freshly-opened blossoms of our beds,

how they ravish us with the sleek marble cocks
that one finds everywhere so mysteriously
broken from the groins of statues. Our wedlocks
are picked by them; we discover in our wives
the seedling sparks from the same fireworking shocks

that bomb-bursted through our body's every cell.
As children, we prayed to be their wards, wanting
them to column night's galleries that fell
around us, to atlas the magically seen-through
skies of our rooms. We were not ready for the angel

that nearly alighted on us, dragonflying
over our succumbed bodies, and were surprised
that they had sex, surprised at how much it stings,
surprised by its warmth, and by their tongues inside
our mouths repeating their fluttering wings.

He's Leaving Home

My image is a thin tin glaze
on the window of the bus;
beyond that, Pittsburgh, with its skyscrapers, hills,
rivers, bridges, and mills, is a bold design
that crosses me out. There, at the rim,
behind the plate glass doors of the terminal,
Mother stands, arm raised in a white pantomime

of surrender. I want to flee
the bus, rush into her arms,
feel the unfinished boyhood flow into my life;
no, I want to be free. Before she has time
to walk to the streetcar, I will be out,
out on the highway; before she reaches home,
opens the door, steps in, switches on the light

on emptiness, we will cross
the county line. As it goes dark,
the towns will be not so much scenes for a ghost
as a palimpsest on which a new profile
of me is being written in white.
From time to time I will turn and see my face,
pale and uncertain, floating along the night.

Shopping for Underwear at Woodward & Lothrop

It is an orchard: the racks
bloom white against dark brown, navy against ivory, red
against tan. The wineskins bulge
with the most exquisite fruits. The scants
are so sheer they barely hold
their peaches. Suddenly, amidst all this choice,
the finest of finery, a slim young man
appears. He searches the branches for briefs,
the low-rise breeches, and I see those swatches tight
on him and go wild with my own ideas. His eyes
flash through shadows and my eyes are mulled

in all their spice. He is north
and I am south or I am north and he is south
but the force works, the force works
as we round each other as we round
the racks in ever tighter turns.
My heart beats so hard it starts to knock the meal
from its wings. I am close enough to reach for him.
But then my safe self wins and I shy
away. From the aisle I watch him peel back his pants
to check the size and I catch sight of a swath
of his brown. And all my body burns.

On the Verandah

A screened porch. The house was old, crumbling, condemned,
soon to be razed to make way for an arid
marble annex to the Library of Congress.
As summer started to steam, we found refuge there.
Whoever came to the front door felt mild airs
lap his cheek as we opened it, was bound to hear
ice chunk against the inside of a Libby glass

pitcher from back of the house, three rooms away,
no matter what time of day. A huge fig tree
spread gluey, dog-scented shadows through the yard,
drenched the porch in a wavery undersea
only candleflecks of sunlight could get through.
It stuck the hand-shaped prints of its leaves on parts
of our bodies as we played we were plaster casts poured

from famous Greek statues. There was one blank wall
across the yard from us, high fences on both sides,
no one to see us. We would vaseline our skin,
strike poses, make love straddling a kitchen chair,
you riding my lap, I sometimes riding yours,
fall asleep after on the wicker settee,
a thin Kashmir shawl shrouding our crossed fallen

limbs. We were living the Southern Decadence
we read about, took long, hot baths, ate peaches
in the nude, drinking the juice from each other.
I did not care for the warm tallow that held us
together, the incense, the chants, the Tantric poses
you would assume, though I could stroke your back for hours,
the breath of my mouth softly ruffling your hair.

A Soft White Room

A white cat curls around one end of it.
We were sitting on a traffic island, too drunk
to walk, when, slow and sleek and still, a white car
    stopped, a man's voice purred, and we got in.
    Now we slump in fur, you at the head,
I on the haunch, the cove of white caracul
between us swarming up and foaming underfoot.
    The man, nude beneath white muslin, hands
prisms to us; through the crystal, I see white
    refracted, and through my touch it clouds
with blue-white brilliance. The man sits. His first kiss
    frosts my lips to his. He thrusts his tongue
    deep into my mouth and I suck ice.

    Down, down, down into the shag I sink.
The man is stripping me and I clutch through wool
down into the scalp. My skin is white, but now
    I look man-dark, man-dark and therefore strong,
    against the blue-white fur, the blue-white wool,
the man's white body inside its sheer white jallaba.
A cat is licking me from instep to groin.
    No, there are two cats. Now you are there,
side-by-side with the man, two tongues and four hands
    worked as one beast. I never liked you.
As the man backs off to focus, I feel your flesh,
    sex for the first time heightened by hate,
    my memory heightened by photoflash.

Red Moon over Mycenae

Think of a big brass cymbal rinsed in blood.
That is what I thought of as the curator spoke,
   his hands with their undeciphered lines
   moving eloquently back and forth
across the tablecloth in boustrophedon
   fashion. My wineglass stopped; the last mouthful
clotted as he described that pendulum's growth

   above the haystacked hills, its strokes spilled
on the back and flanks of a naked Greek youth
   who was crouching in the presumed spot
   where Electra came out to greet sweet
air, his head drowning in sainthood when he stood
   into the moon. My breath shook as his breath
shook, as though swallowed by the night's windless flute,

   when the youth's white figure moved across its red
clay background; he was watching one of the jugs
   he had restored come to life within his grasp
   and I was watching an image live
again as he restored it. I was made part
   of that museum through the sway of words.
For one moment I was very close to love.

Shopping for Peaches on Second Avenue

Summer sets in on us. Sundogs roam
the streets, their heat woofing up to where we hang
at night, too ragged to sleep. All around St. Mark's Place
the drum of the sun goes on, the hulls
that once were buildings melted to scrap
inside their boxwork. It is a war zone: tanks
roll out the small of the morning as we start
awake, the ceiling burning in blue jets
above us. In the evenings we sit
the stoops, riding on sheer animus the straits
too far from us for comfort, their salt
too faint for us to smell. Jason sits
with us, his golden fleece the white gold
of his hair, the medieval red gold of his flesh.
Puerto Rican boys pass by, each one Hylas called

out to his Hercules. Their eyes rave
at us as they walk our way. Looks boomerang
back as Jason smiles and butterflies each face
and dazzles off. In one of the lulls
between boys, someone suggests a fruit
and Jason says, "Peaches," remembering red flanks
along the trees, not peaches but mangoes, but sick
with the same sweet juice. Jason forgets
the flavor of a peach. As we pick
through, though, he knows the pubescent feel of them,
their downy blond pinkness. We stand there transfixed
as the magic inflames our mouths, pure sun
distilled in teenager's skin. The mess
runs down and off of us as we bend to bite
at another piece of fruit, each bite a kiss.

Men as Tall as El Greco's Men

My body turns out as twisted white with flash
     as *San Sebastián*, muscles wrung
from wax, two white dabs on the chest, a whitejack
squeezed from the groin. This is not his fashion sketch,
     a horse's legs kicking under silk
until it gives off sparks, but it is as grand,
as vain, as artificial. Fifteen years pass
        and we climb a building's shell
     past doorways black with the rooms below
and up the rungs of stairways to his room. Big top,
     the roof hangs his sideshow at one end:

the werewolves, the bearded ladies, the tallest men
     in the world of his life: and these are
the fashion kings, the manikin-men and, yes,
the famous callboys of New York. They are wed
     to the wall in the very cheapest paints,
the ugly/beautiful, the beautiful/ugly, glad
with polychrome until the wrecking-ball hits
       and paint flits into the street.
     And then I see: larger than the rest,
painted from that highschool sketch of me, a saint
     to kneel to in the chancel of his bed.

All Saints' Day

The sun breaks the window, cuts across the bed,
  and wets your face. I see muzzle, long gray eyes,
red-gold pelt. You are fox in the morning. Your range is wide,

rounding me out the way a scalp-reader will.
  We float in the thaw, legs trailing down, hands tied.
Last night we floated on air, two of you a while

on either side, a magic trick. The other one
  was wilier than you, more winning, dread wolf
but drunk. Then Paul came in, not quite so dark with wine

as us, and wheedled him out. We were strangers. A wish
  was in your heart, though, and craft, as you weighed there
in the heart of this old house, an old pang set to push

both of us forward. I came through the long-strewn
  Jacobean chairs, past the grit-blue Canton ware,
under the raftered pewter tankards. You were then

before the portrait of the host, our friend. As we met,
  his eyes – even those painted eyes – picked at us.
But you were guest, you had a bed, we could forget

the masquerade, shed our old lives as we shed the cloth
  of our costumes, come out of us as the sun rides
this morning, God's new men, saints ourselves or gods.

A Photograph of You in Greece

You are leaning against the bottom fifth
of a ruined column, standing on the plinth.
   The Acropolis is in the background.
Your hair was all red then and as you pause, arms
   braced against the broken top of the piece,
    the sun that lights the right half of your face,
so that you squint slightly, makes your hair too dark,
darker than I remember it, with a few glints
   of gold. You gave me this photograph
right after we met, hoping perhaps to catch
   with me if I put it where you could watch,

   ex voto, over me. You did catch,
not by this photograph, but with every branch
   of your temperament – bud, leaflet, bud,
blossom, leaf – until our crowns were part and part
   of each other. We have had our strains
    as we grew, not as the capital grows
into the frieze, but as buckthorns in a park
will grow into an alley. You look at yourself
   and think you are old, and worry. But the staff
of Greece, the sun, shines on you as from the start,
   and you are always new to my heart.

On the Bus to Portland

As soon as I get on, I feel pull
on me. Suited in black, dark blue turtleneck,
        my face and hands must glow white
against the bituminous gloom of the bus, a paint
        artists used to call "mummy". My eyes
especially draw their attention. There is one,
        in back, who is riveted to me.
        I walk hand over hand to where she sits.
She is a witch. She invites me to join her
        at her coven. Weekends – week in, week out –
I trail the coast north from Boston, meeting my life
        on its way down to me. I live there
for one who is a homily for me: homely, plain,

        unmysterious. I thrill to the feel full
of power drawn from earth, moon, stars, at our beck
        banding round in lightning light
us thirteen people. I have a sight of him,
        heavy-sexed, rich with me, and we touch
here in my lap, here in the bus, such is the reach
        of their magic through the woman here
        beside me. I am perfect for them.
That one kiss calls up all my bones to join him.
        But I am the victim of my own
voluptuousness. I gaze ahead at the one
        who waits for me and see strength and care
and peace. No, it is I, I who am the witch.

The Snow Is Falling

La neige renvoie ici au froid,
mais ce n'est pas fatal, c'est même rare:
la neige, manteau moelleux, duveteux,
connote plutôt la chaleur des substances
homogènes,la protection de l'abri.

Roland Barthes

Christmas Eve. The forequarters of night
    were wound in tissue-paper frost. Shrill
moonlight gutted the ground, laying bare
    the dusty ancient bones. Murky trees
arched their tentacles as if to stare

through the weedy waters of the air.
    They are prophesying an open
winter. One of those winters with rags
    of thorny wind scrawling the house, cat's
claws of ice sowing on spars and crags

of the roof, where the lank moonlight snags.
    We looked out before going to bed:
Our faces were pasted on the panes
    like paper lanterns filled with ghost-fire.
Outside was dark, saturated, stains

of raveled shadow tossing like manes.
    The Christmas tree stands in the parlor;
needles of resin spark in its fur.
    You, my sister, you and your husband
sleep in the next room, lulled by a purr

of comforter cats that scarcely stir.
　　　3 o'clock. I am churned out of sleep
by the sleek, satiny whisking fall
　　　of diamond flakes from the jeweler's hand,
steadily stroking window and wall.

And behind that: the ratchet and crawl
　　　of some machine lunging in the road.
I slide the Indian shutters aside:
　　　Wonderland of mica white! Mantle
of sequin snow coating the rough hide

of earth; pearly dove petals that glide
　　　the glassy night, velvety and what? – yes,
downy. Within those several short hours
　　　since I went to bed, snow has mounded –
sudden outburst of candytuft flowers –

more than a foot. Already snow plowers
　　　are clearing it away, and the plow,
huge yellow beetle, blinks alternate
　　　yellow and red, spewing snow to one side.
Night is a lustrous caress: ornate

glove of gems scabbarding duplicate
　　　soft, white hands: silken quilt swaddling
the house with oneness. All is not quite
　　　silent, not quite still – but infinitely
calm, drunk with unwavering inner light.

The Darkest Night of the Year

They were not feathers
but swollen, wet wads of snow
that spattered my sister's brand-new, furless, black
cloth coat. I was half a world away, sprawled in a mild
tropical evening. In the mountains
of Pennsylvania, the first day of winter
is often washed with snow. The heart
is not enhanced by it. No one doubles back

to watch such snow pack
the wounds of a stranger's woods.
A gauze of it was caught on the northern burr
of the mound of earth beside my mother's grave,
but on the flat it melted instants
above the earth's putty, and as my sister
turned aside, I might have seen
her heels stamp fingernail-shaped seals behind her.

At home, she dug spurs
into the phone as she dialed
my number repeatedly. She guessed I lay
in a stranger's arms overnight and could not be reached.
There was no way that grief could touch me
yet. No one could have determined whose passion
was stronger, my sister's or mine,
as she tensely waited for her night, my day.

One Chill Night

Fifteen minutes, perhaps only ten. You sit
in the American Colonial chair-table.
Its nearly oval top has the same effect
as the glory around a graceful Buddhist god.
Footfalls cross. Our only neighbor has not knocked,

refuses to know I'm about to depart.
Snow squeals and cracks beneath his path as he draws
certainly away. If he turns – but he will not –
and glances through the wavery water-shaped glass,
he'll see me stoop to clutch the dog, clasp each cat

tightly enough to press their warm indifferent
bodies indelibly forever into the earth
of my heart. He would see me glance one last time
jealously around the room to fix the shape
of it, as if I knew I'd never see the same

room again; he would not see the unfamiliar sting
in your eyes as you rise to concede my passing
and would look aside as your face bends to mine,
his heart numbed, as ours are, by ice or a trace
of scalding, but definitely full of pain.

Kagurazaka Station

Time: 3 min.

       Neither our minds nor our commands
will forward the poem.
                   Poetry has its lines
    of four feet or five feet or six feet
which move along according to the contour
       of their meter, and they may
    not be hurried.
                   The train's sleeve – sheath or sleeve –
is quilted with 3 in. sq. tiles of impure

    aquamarine shaded gray,
green, blue, in a retrospective show of Yüeh
    celadons.
          Length, width, vault of the roof,
suggest nothing so much as Perry High School pool
       with Phidias' *Naked Athlete*
    poised at one end of it, prepared to leap
into the poem's variable waters.
              The rule

    of "form" toward which an object
tends is the poem's sleeve.
            Though the arm is free
    to move where it will, it is not free
of the sleeve, which molds its motion around the spine
       of it, waving totally
    sovereign dancer's fingers at its end,
now flowers on a satin stem.
            We align

the train with the flow of its veins;
we name it by the heat of its pulse.

It turns
around its stations' nodes as the pace
of the poem is drawn through its knots of rhyme.

It is measured.

It has space
and from space it acquires motion,
from motion it has time.

Court music, too, has time.

It is marked by the hiccup
of the drum, the clack of the *shakubyoshi*,
"clappers".

The train's windows are paper'd
with black-capped, black-suited high school boys.

They have wings
and angels' faces.

The doors
open on the highly formal music
as through the vacant car the diver strides

and springs.

Various Ways of Interpreting a Street

To the young man in the ink-blue kimono
returning from the bath, the rain that lines the street
    simply prolongs the glaze of water
on the tiles of the bath, the veil of moisture
that hovers around his still-steaming body,

    the film on the soles of his bare feet
sticking his palm-smooth paulownia-wood *geta*
    fast to them for part of a second
each time he lifts his feet. From the angle of his eyes
to all possible points along the surface

    of the street, lights reflected on it,
also the canes of the weeping willow tree
    growing beside it, do not appear
as long wavery lines to him, making it seem
to be the eye-black water of a canal,

    as it does to the man looking down
from his second-floor balcony. The illusion
    would be complete if the man would tilt
his head from one side to the other, so the wet
with its trails of white shimmering in it would flow,

    actually flow, from right to left. The willow
might be growing on a bank. The bell-ring insect
    clutching at the rye grass at its foot
fears the wet plain of the street, as though it were
water, the unlit blotches in it the shadows

certain great gray fish make as they hang
inside it; it will not leap. As soon as the young man
   in the ink-blue kimono wades into sight,
the street ceases to be water. If he looks
up at the face of the man on the balcony

   he will see a child's face at the instant
the child first realizes he has been lost,
   beneath that the speechless ecstasy
the male sockeye salmon must know as he scales
the female, feelings that are clear but have no name.

Please Do Not Walk on the Pigeons.
Do Not Feed the Grass.

In Montparnasse's back alleys we still seem to see
her, that recurrent bag lady, Gertrude Stein,
scavenging the scuffed and broken bric-a-brac
of unloved words: those concatenated verbs
with their chubby syllables, like beads of fine

German sausage, pleasing to the palate
if not to the eye. And the flat adjectives,
so flat and so spare, so uncompromisingly
English, but in their Englishness something odd,
atavistic, alien, posed as substantives

in their children's-book colors, swiping the starch
from the outfit of their nominal neighbors.
Up the street with her tautological step
she strides, strides along at a tongue-twisting pace.
We attempt to follow, fond of her labors,

but soon she shakes us, ducking down a backhand
byway. We have come to another impasse.
The street sign here reads: *Non Sequitur*, the same
address where pigeons strut about, I guess, strut
and shout "hooray!" while poets mostly shout "alas!"

Among the Lisu of Northern Thailand

"Byootiful!" They know one English word
and say it, "Byootiful! Byootiful!"
    as they overrun our car,
pressing upon us their women's handicraft,
    small blocks of concentric squares
    done in much the same manner as pieced quilts.
I'm not here to buy. I want their vernacular

    for a Conspectus of Lolo-Burmese,
    their myths, their sagas. I pay ten *baht*
    per person for a round dance,
twenty *baht* to the player of the *khen*, a mouth
    organ composed of long reeds
    arranged in a fasces plan. Children
press their pig's noses against the elegance

    of my camera's crystal-ball lenses.
    By the time I wipe off their grimaces
    the dance has come to an end
and must be paid for again. The women sit
    on one raised covered platform;
    sew, smoke, and chat, while the men play cards,
smoke, and chat on another platform. Unpenned

    chickens and ducks peck over the rice
    spread in the compound to dry. No one
    is in the fields. They are not
an industrious people. One old woman,
    now using the one old tooth
    of the Graiae, says she has sagas
to sell, holds out one sun-gloved hand. My snapshot

still holds still the quaver of her mouth;
my tapes hold the quaver of her voice.
But no grammar holds the quirk
of her words as her tale unfolds across cold
martinis at seven, smooth
brown fingers caressing my bare back,
as I leave to a different man the fieldwork.

In my Breast, Something Marked "Fragile"

It is not what the Chinese call "sand rats", or jerboa,
    west of Khotan running after their horses,
although it jumps so, as the hawk rides lower

and lower in its almost exhausted sky.
      You can hear the clicking of their prayer-bead eyes
as the nothing-left-to-hide-in forces

them from hiding in their unreeling spools of life.
    The horses turn, veer, steer like a stallion-prowed
regatta across the horizon that overlies

in unbroken emptiness breakers of sand:
    they're four-gaited and tall and their hooves make
                  the world's last
music. The eyes of the rats now know that the crowd

of strange cadences they so admired has hunters'
    responsibilities, that horses have their hawks.
Tomorrow their monkey-puzzle bones will be broadcast

on the campfired sand like white calligraphy
    and, in the midst of such carelessly strewn words,
you may find something more compelling that talks

with its hands: shards of an artifact once clay
    but burned to the hardness of ice in the slow
cone-5 fire above the desert. Then, one day,

a curator of Inner Asian Art will say rough
    clay like this should have been fired in a milder way
or was not in the kiln nearly long enough.

Going by Horsecart

to Than Zaw U

The tawny plain behind us stretches
   in its own dust and yawns; between its paws
a mousy village struggles to free its groves.
   In front of Tourist Burma, a fleet
   of Pennsylvania Dutch dower chests
waits for us. We are won by lot. I am drawn
   by a fourteen-year-old boy. He boasts

   that his horse, his cart, are best. I settle
   among the frakturwork tulips. My shell
opens and its monarch flits out. This drab land
   is the magic green powder witch doctors use;
   my sorrow is cured by it. My guide's skin
is the color of Roman copper coins unearthed
   in China; his smile flowers from its tan

   in fast motion, an entire season
   forced into a few seconds. We have time
to touch hearts before we reach the first brick spire
   in a tableland full of vials,
   which king's vanity? The guide reveals
a spot from which Buddha's lips seem to curve up,
   elation reaching across the dark aisles.

Assault with Intent to Kill

It was about the size of a nickel – no,
the size of a dime – pressed against my temple,
and cold. At first it was only that, the cold,
I could consider, how unpleasant it was,
nuzzling through the short hairs, against the temporal nerve,
where only a week before the Hong Kong barber
stroked with his clippers, the last person in the world

to touch me. Gradually, as the warmth of my skin
unfolded by convection into the metal,
I was aware of the smoothly rounded ring
that was the lip of the barrel, considered
its bore, the exact diameter of the hole
that the bullet, fired from that distance, would drill
through my head. Another man would feel lifelong

pleasures pour across his mind, which you have heard
a drowning man gains as he thirstily sucks
the last thin airs of life. I could only think
of the pain my death would bring to someone I love,
the uselessness. Imagine my quiet as the hand
that held the gun shuddered, drawing it away,
veered in a wide arc and sighted it pointblank

at my sister. I could not make out his face,
but I knew by the tone color of his voice
he was clenching his teeth, hard, when he described
with intimate hunter's knowledge how her brains
would erupt from her skull as soon as he pulled
the trigger. Within two feet of her ear, he fired.
She did not flinch. The shot leapt into the soft wood

of the window frame. If the neighbors heard that shot
and looked across, they must have seen the precise
scalene triangle formed by the three of us,
one brother, two sisters, seated at the ellipse
of the dining table, the infinite vectors
which the brother-in-law was making with respect
to the focus of that ellipse and the transverse

axis determined by the three fixed at each
vertex of the triangle, by the slightest
modulation in facial features, by every tinge
of error in our speech. They must have seen us waiting
for them to call the police, waiting in vain,
waiting for a counterweight in chance, minute
but meaningful, waiting for something to change.

Forster Arrives in Dewas Senior

This is no way to dress. Cuffs frayed, shirtfront grayed
    by the local penitential stream
where Baldeo washed as he washed Forster's linen,
no amount of snipping would make this wardrobe
    sing. The trip over was in high style;
    the Maharajah of Indore's car
slinked between the tattooed elephants with fire

in its nostrils and a very throaty roar,
    but the great white houseguests who got out
were as rumpled as though they had ridden by rail.
He was about to descend to the banquet
    with gutter on his knees when the king
    himself came in with piles of gold sleeves
and leggings. At first nothing fit. "He who gives

garments to a beggar will be clothed with the sun."
    One household must have outshone the rest,
for they sent up the shirts off their backs, the pants
off their lower limbs. Let him describe himself:
    white muslin jodhpurs, a waistcoat striped
    like a Neapolitan ice, a coat
of claret-colored silk trimmed with gold and – not quite

the thing for dabbing away sweat – an orange silk
    scarf with gold ends to hold in his left hand.
A tintype taken at the time does not show
this heady *macédoine* of color. The young
    dandy *malgré lui* looks out from the worn
    backdrop tentatively, loved not as hard
as he had hoped, but permanently adored.

Oh, Calcutta

The town-plan is British: squares, circles, parks.
    It is Cleveland left to rot
one hundred years and occupied by bronzes,
    though Cleveland's streets are not caked with earth
and piled with coconuts. Beggars hunch in rags;
    ladies mince across the muck in silks
a Roman empress would have envied. A guide lurks

    in the entryway of my hotel;
        he wants to take me by cab,
even on foot. At Kali temple a glimpse of fat
    between fingers is said to be her eye.
A sari shop is more inviting. A Greek
    statue, but nearly black, kneels in bloods
and fires and wines. His shirt is ripped; nothing hides

    the fig-skin of his chest. He serves rum.
        It makes the guide deceptive
but I grow bold; only the guide's gaze stops me
    from reaching forward to pluck a piece
of human fruit. Outside, the sun spreads such wares
    in every street; lesser gods rise wet,
gleaming, naked, from the gutter at my feet.

How All Eyes Become One

As I lift the mask of your face
between my fingers as though to drink
from it, a lioness in Etosha turns
into a snarling patch of desert as she digs
herself into the throat of the one she wants.
At that very moment, your springbok's eyes
swim up at me, surrendering, surprised.
High above the earth, in their warm cocoon of air,
hundreds of eyes exactly the same size

clutch at the cliffs above them
as the spider's claws of a fighter plane
splinter their bodies. I wanted to kiss you.
The hem of your kimono-heavy hair folds
along my forearms. I am too weak to lift it.
I never knew that particular
encumbrance to his limbs the ravisher
must feel as he edges forward for the kill.
I never knew how very frightened you are.

What Happened in the Barabar Caves

The day goes blue and blue and blue as the train
    clicks along its abacus towards the sun,
first the blue of peacocks' necks, then the blue, blue frit
    that glasses the skulls of mosques,
and then the bluets blue that runs in arabesques
through every courtyard's tiles. Blue? Not blue by eight,
    but white, white when the sun racks its mouth
and fizzes. With sun blades crashing on his back,
    Forster toeholds the pigeon-toed path

up toward the grottoes. *Camera obscura*, on one wall
    of which the whole poisoned plain below
is mirror'd in miniature and upside-down,
    the cave has him in its lens
when he steps through, much as Aziz will step through,
in out of the light, and he sees his bat self
    hanging, lifting its arms/spreading its wings.
Just at bell center, a great Amen! of thoughts
    breaks from him and reverberates in gongs

from one bell-metal surface to the other. Come!
    it calls loud enough to call a god.
True to his word, the stones' webbed roses and grays
    come alive in candlepower:
we light a match and see the three of us fanned
into a fossil existence in the stone,
    moth'd and wavering and, beneath us, the forms
of two men, one with Forster's face, his body arched,
    ringed from behind in a new god's arms.

Wanting to Turn into a Wolf

Those almond-cut topaz eyes
you see at night crutched in a corner
of your room will hopefully be mine.
    If you dare, you will make out,
as your flashlight slices into me, a form
that still remembers how to stand, balancing
    on two hind paws, delicately upright

    for the moment, but staggering
as though taxed by its cobweb-colored wool.
The mind quickly releases its hold
    on the shape of all five fingers, drops
me to my forefeet as you flee, as I leap
and follow, still knowing your name but baying
    as a hound bays. The jaggèd beast that lopes

    after you has little of me
left in it. I will want you to lurch
and scream as I overtake your sleigh,
    the windy kite-strings it unreels
across the snow flowered with my own paw prints,
I will want you to throw your boys out to me,
    will tenderly lick their fingernails

    the nooks of their eyes, though I do not
know why, before I bend to eat the breath
from their throats. I will not stop, though you send
    me foot-bound geese, venison, push
the agèd coachman overboard toward me. I shall rush
on, blizzard-blind, lapping the whet of your cries,
    I want that first sweet shock of your flesh.

Sometimes in the Night the Truth Comes

Your analyst says, "Anger
need not be destructive," but it destroys us,
ugly heads that rise and hiss at us;
the more we try to still them, the more we stir
them up. You are a person of some patience.
And you are mild. My guilt should melt
in your silence rather than growing worse.

Yet, sometimes at night I wake
and press the shadow of my hand across your throat.
Only the moon witnesses my crime
but you move and moan as though choked. Your face cools
like a child's face under sleep. I am too tame
to kill you. Suddenly a look
of utter helplessness dims the room.

What is Written in Windows

How many years I have loved you, and not known
    that I loved you, or how much, or why,
I cannot say. Waking and thinking of you
    is not extraordinary; having the sky
fill my arms with bolts of you, a bright festoon

with your face and your body printed on it
    as I reach for morning through the pool
of my window is a daily feat. If it is vice
    or madness to drink up your image
from the surface of mirrors or to kiss

empty statues thinking that you stay in them,
    then I am mad and vicious. The frames
of casements, pictures, whatever houses glass,
    may have your presence floating on it.
Museum cases have learned how to express

you, the waxworks or the mummies hung inside
    offering you the room to stand or sit
with them, your smile, the tilt of your head above
    their unoccupied bodies haunting
them as you haunt me, remarkably alive.

Space Walk

In space, there is neither up nor down.
The earth, at first the sleek silk lining
    in a great lute-bellied dome,
      stippled with lapis lazuli to portray
one of Tiepolo's skies with plump cupids' legs
      diving through it, next suddenly turns
      upside down into a brilliant ozone

    pond or the underlit marble-glass floor
    of a fashionable discotheque.
        The skywalker literally flows
      from the hatch and teeters across a tightrope
anchored to one of the mirror'd pinwheel wings
      of the space station; he waves his limbs
      slowly, ungracefully, as though the four

    were eight, as though he were a trap-door
    spider using the web-spider's nylon
        ladder. This white cotton doll
      on television moves, not by unseen strings
but by very primitive clockwork; sidewalk
      vendors sell tiny boulevardiers
      that move faster than he does. Matador

    in an airy arena, he struts forth
    against the charging star-stuff
        with a mantle of man-made fur
      to shield him. He gazes up at the grandstand
where the hometown sits and glimpses the northern lights
      like a crown above it. Only he
      knows there is a halo around the earth.

A Voice from the Past

At two o'clock in the afternoon,
as I was searching for a seat at Renoir,
    someone there called, "Roger!" There was no one
I knew, only the black-haired ones, their heads bent
    over coffee, no blond, no one looked up.
That was a dead man's voice. My vigil was at an end,
    though it was difficult to watch,
from such a distance, friend, near-friend, swell with gift,
    his body an ant mine catacombed
    with passages. Oh, we were tomfooled
    by each other, they all knew that,
they knew we were upstairs in the old rope bed
dialing down to Flo's Steamed Dogs, his bosom gemmed,

    the countess calling, his hand
on his throat wattling his voice into a whir,
    for enough steamed dogs for a sit-down
for forty, perfectly dowager. We were fun
    for a while, but much too cousin. My cup
cools around its coffee as I look from the floor above
    the street at the same gray street
in the same gray day I have seen so many times
    here. I did not realize
    that day that he had died, just as he called
    to me, really one o'clock
the night before, his time. I sit here and hear
his voice again, as only the loved one does.

Leaving Miyajima

The sea is not really silver.
The ship swerves, breaking the goldleaf in its wake
into millions of rolling silver-skinned fry
    or phosphorescent plankton.
Just to the right of Itsukushima shrine
  there is always smoke, some small
factory. No artist could have planned a finer vein

    to veil that monotonous part
of the mountainside. The sun swords down through it,
flaring like the gilt sticks of an old lace fan.
    The gate in front of the shrine
wades lava. You hold your hands over the rail
  as though to warm them in that radiance
or warn the priests that flame is spreading downhill.

    You are strewing wishes. You want
to come back some day, and wonder if you will.
We are suspended between light and quicksilver.
    To you this means "mirror". For me,
it is the world's heaviest liquid. I am held
  in it. The hours we spent here fireflower
behind us, though it is January and I am chilled.

Arriving in Venice

As the train nears Venice, the city unfolds
   on its stem like the fairy flowers
that schoolchildren invent, matchless but unmatched
   wings added arbitrarily, one
after one, as though the thousand-petal'd form
the yogi managed to balance on his spine
   suddenly went haywire, or a blown

glass lily erupted in long candy frills
   at the end of its tube. This is a dream
I have had for more than thirty years, the stairs
   moored underwater, black lacquer swans
bowing their prows, inviting us to lie in.
The black swans are really there, but I am caught
   crossfire in haggling, compelled to sit

aboard the vaporetto, my body trapped
   in my own luggage. The water assumes
the color of plasticene. The boat is bound
   the wrong way round, past parking. And yet,
as San Marco's domes, coppery emeralds set
in an old and neglected bronze ring, emerge
   above goldwork, dreams and truth converge.

The "Bird-of-Prey and Prey" Motif

True, the art of the steppes
    is monumental, though miniature.
The Ordos bronze plaques – what are they, pendants, charms,
    toggles, brooches, clasps? – take on the stance
of bas-reliefs when published side-by-side with them.
There is a big-horned sheep among them, moosey faced,
    a little heavy, his horns
acting out the arabesque that starts in the cock
to his tail, his feet tethered to each other's posts
at the base, a finial, that is at its best
    beside Degas' bronze horse. A hedgehog stomps
    in place, his burbles spaced so evenly
we think it is its modern paraphrase. The bronze was danced

into all these shapes,
    not poured, the billies crested and cocksure,
the tigers fighting a flirting flyting fight, arms
    about each other. Here, a bird of prey
dives into a stag, there two of the birds maim
a wolf. Atkinson in his travels has drawn
    both these scenes from life, "Bearcoots
and Wolves" and "Bearcoots Attacking a Steinbock," in wondrous
detail, birds' bills tearing up the ghosts
of the beasts, tearing at the liver. The taste
    is what the poet tastes as his beast self tramps
    beneath his bird self, his shaman self, his ecstasy
lasting as long with him as they last their pain.

In the Picture None of Us Are Missing

You reel back from the phone as though slapped.
Why am I so afflicted?
It was your brother who died.
I roam the house, helpless as a child,
staring into shadows. My arms will not lift
their own weight. Six months ago we sailed
down the Rhine. Some of the scenes we photographed

are in the camera, the dead man's face
imminent, undeveloped,
still full of life. When the slides
come back, you will see the two of us
there on the deck, his arm around my shoulders.
Both of us will be smiling. I missed
having a brother all these years. My childhood prayers

always included someone like him
to care for me, yet no one
who sees this picture will think
we are brothers. How long will this chill
go on stabbing me? I should learn from his love
to be a brother, brace you with my arms
and comfort you, though I have no comfort to give.

Seen through the Window of a Car

Slow, slow, dream-slow, the young man
wipes the palm leaf up his arm
and leaves a trail of muck there. Two children stare
at him squatting at the gutter posed
for washing and I stare as our car
rounds into Rantepao and I see him dream
himself into washing dip the leaf
into the gutter and draw it toward his skin.
The driver and the man beside me have seen

and have turned their heads or they
have not seen. But their heads are turned.
Passers-by squint at the young man loined in rags,
top half bare, but they frown and move on.
The young man dreams and dips the leaf again.
Only the children and I will dare to look
at him. We wonder if this time, this time
he will lift it to his face. The car
breaks traffic. Only the children know for sure.

Forster Visits T. E. Lawrence at Clouds Hill

They kneel on pile over old pine planks.
The light, laced with fresh elm green
laced with the evergreen of rhododendrons, melts
the madders and the indigos beneath them
into stained glass. Lawrence's book drifts
in dunes about them. Old elm logs utter reds
in the fireplace, goldleafing both men's hair.
There's a hair's breadth between these men
finer than their own hair, a string that, when played,
sounds so high that only beasts hear. For Forster, Love
is God; for Lawrence, Satan. For Forster, all
is possible. At lunch – cold chicken and ham,
stewed pears and cream, "very nice and queer" –

Forster stares out the window past wilds
of rhododendrons and sees sands rise
in dust devils on Thomas Hardy's Dorset;
he sees Dahoum embodied for the first time
beneath Lawrence's kisses. Well, it makes
a fine tale. He must promise to come again
before Lawrence allows him to leave,
and they set a date. On May
the 13th, on the way back from Bovington Camp,
Lawrence ran his motorcycle off the road
and was killed. He passed from a world without love
to a world without God. It was the next day
that Forster was scheduled to arrive.

As in Yogyakarta the *Becak* Drivers Dream

As in Yogyakarta the *becak* drivers curl
　　　　　　in their shadowy cocoons,
I slide into a taxi in Taksim Square
in Istanbul: they drowse through the cocktail hour
　　　　　　　of the tourist, the home time
　　　　of stockbrokers; twilight swings in droves
beneath the champak trees and the unbottled scent
　　　　　in the flowers drives the drivers to dream
of odd Thousand-and-One-Nights places where mosques glow gold
beside elegant waters; or, there is rain,
and it beads with the rightness of a metronome

from the overhanging boughs. There is no rain here.
　　　　　　The taxi delves straight downhill
toward a spread of glitter banked by a heightened prose
bristling with spires. Your letter yields, "I miss you.
　　　　　I love you," inside my hands,
　　　　stronger than the talk of three backseat friends.
The city below – old, obscure, opulent –
　　　　melts at once beneath an aftermath
of your city with you in it. Excitement
is not here. Even the palaces of God
are not nearly breathless enough without your breath.

Triple By-Pass

"Poor wretch," I think, "poor wretch," as they wheel him round
       in white, on white, round the door
    and down the long white causeway. Down there
we watched his heart in cloud chamber, its blocked walls
       black against gray breaking beat by beat;
    I scanned the screen and saw a small bird
bucking its way deeper into a trap. I press
       my lips to my palm and press my palm
    to his cheek; the kiss goes a long way down
    into his whiteness, goes straight for the heart.
They wheel him through the great white doors, beneath a board

he cannot read, and I know I have lost him.
       I know then I have lost him.
    Our enemies will tinker with him
and he will die under the knife. Ten o'clock,
       noon, two o'clock, four o'clock, six. Numb,
    I huddle in the chill blow of his room,
the chill November wind squealing across slate
       on his windows. His birthday is soon.
    I am not strong enough to think, "If he dies . . ."
    Yes, I have wished him dead and the words
rankle along the room. The light is very dim

around me now and when the nurse comes to take me
       to him the white blinds me, the white,
    pure white of Intensive Care blinds me;
but I see him there, his head snapped to one side,
       his body in block and tackle, hose,
    hose everywhere hooking him to life.
I start, "Live, live, live," a litany, but my mouth
       is raw and sounds crack out to the stare
    of all the doctors. They have broken him
    in two, I see, but they have saved him,
all their knives easier on him than my knife.

61

Dancing Bear

That was the one thing in Istanbul I did not see.
    Down there, down there, down Silverwater Street,
    the fur man came, came and danced for you,
his great head swinging left then right; his great arms
out to you. Skinned, a bear is human. This bear's dance
    was an oom-pah-pah to clarinets,
the dozey-do Renoir has stopped in mid-step
    so suddenly that the woman in pink
and her partner brink on breaking from the brush-strokes.
    One more whirl, and the bear would waltz you
    deep into the artist's world, jack's box.

One month later, you lay in the white room, skinned
    to the heart. You told me about the bear.
    Your voice was so worn I heard halftones, saw halftones,
heard my great-great-grandfather speak
through you, saw the engraving in one of his books,
    Travels in Turkey, the dancing bear
a badge of fur against fur sky, a furry mosque,
    and I was envious. Dancing bear,
dancing bear, get up and dance with me. Fireworks,
    fountains, I want that summer with you
    again, or six of those seven weeks.

The 12:30 Bus to Narita Airport

The bus slips
    from the curb and his face suns with it.
    Buildings on this side of the street slip
across the windows, their windows filled with sky
writing out his face with their whiteness, his wave
    fainting down to nothing behind the glare.
      I turn and stare at strangers.
    I will never love any of them.
I push through puppets, my own face skinned alive,

my last chance
    to catch at the bus as it turns, turns,
    blocked by them, their strings tangled, their heads
unturned, unfinished, blank. It is Sunday. I walk
our Sunday walk down to the park. There I run
    from hiding place to hiding place, too stunned
      to call to him. The dangers
    are even greater at home, his clothing gone,
half of everything in every drawer withdrawn.

Room by room
    I wash off the tracks of missing things.
    The walls that were closing in on us
now shrink away from me, leaving me alone
at the center of a very small space. Time and time
    again my hands stop dead. I see him
      turn toward the bus, the changes
    that have happened to us evident in his look,
and I tear with pain. But he is going home.

The Far Corners Closes Its Doors

It was my idea, the shop.
No, it was yours. "Museum quality stuff,"
the dealers sniffed, but America
was suddenly Third World, banks
were closing, Gentiles were sleeping on the ground,
no one was buying. We fold
the flying carpets, break chests-on-chests
of all their boxy magic, pack in
the Oriental apparatus. It was fanfare!
when we opened, ribbon cutting, the mayor mad
for our elegance in that part of town.

Wrong time, wrong place. Five of us
stretch across a photograph. Your face is much too old
for me, white with fear, your eyes quirky
for the future. You held on
to it for less than a year. As the walls go blank
again, I know how you sat
day after day hurting a piecemeal hurt
as you watched each day empty to its end.
Think of the loss. Your savings of thirteen years.
And yet you are home. The success that we planned
would have brought me out of the wrong land.

Corps de Ballet

These boys are thugs, really, hush
and husky. It is summer and the great doors
　　　are open. Light fans in with the wind,
　　　billowing the sheer white sails that hang
　　　the windows. One boy is at the barre
across the room. An aurora borealis skims
　　　between us, alternately veiling him
　　　and unveiling him, naked to the waist.
Inside this cocoon, his body is bud-hard,
　　　bud-wet, his skin glistening with a net
　　　of lighter brown as the sun plays up
the watery weave over the shoals of his skin.
　　　He spreads his arms in a harp

　　　above his head and his build
opens welterweight into a rose with its bloom
　　　in a century of petals. His legs
　　　are almost obscene inside their trunks,
　　　so heavy are they with muscles; his moves
are flowery, though, as his thighs open and shut,
　　　open and shut, cutting their way through
　　　the cloth of the music. I have brought
with me an aphrodisiac from Turkey. I unclench
　　　my fist to him when the other boys have gone.
　　　He rubs the rouge from my hand, my palm,
and tastes it. I see his face, my face, his face,
　　　my face reach by mirror no end to them.

Through This Window

Through this window I cannot gaze across my fields
         into the break in my woods
         where the lair of the deer is.
     I cannot hear the foghorn's woo! and woo!
     as the sea sighs toward the shore its mists
         and the mists walk the river
     and waver on the edge of my land.
But I see mountains in fleet, their sharp sails raked
breaking the sky, and I see the eighth-hour mist
spinning up onto the sun's spools from last night's drench.
I walk and sing but my song is heavy with the past

and does not lift. I am happy with my new terrain,
         but it is not home. The hills peak
         raggedly in cypresses;
     the birds are brisk but they have no names;
     even the moon, that follower, is odd,
         too milky and much too mild;
     it is not the moon of home. An artist
of this place would paint me dense and dark and small
against bare room, and I would fit his boundaries,
but I do not belong. I want to live large
and very bright. I want to be where my heart is.

Home Stay

Domain is what I see when I walk out,
cup in hand, on the green-gold silks the sun flings
   through the grass. The zest of coffee blends
      with the mead of phlox, white phlox,
   man-high here in the sun, the bolls tight
and loose as cloud cover, immense with coolness.
I stand on stone – a terrace – and watch the shards
   in a ruined English border brood
back on the seasons: peonies have passed; mourning bride

   hangs dark with tatters; globe thistles quill
steel blue inside a round of goldfinches' wings.
   The hues I have restored bloom out loud
      in the fresh sweep of spaces; some glee
   now but the June favorites I shall not see
until a Sabbath year. As I veer the lawn
past apple gnarl behind new windflower pink,
   the man in the house looks out at me across a bed
that will go starry when I leave and break into seed.

A Voice from on High

As I round the frieze barefoot,
barefoot to grip the ledge, your voice floats down.
One of the gandharvas I am photographing
must have spoken. I stand to see and it is you
there, beyond the wall, your eyes
behind sunglass gazing at me. You are here
without me. Last night I heard you tell
what you would not tell in letters. As your words
worked closer and closer to the truth
they meant less and less to me. At last, I cast you
from our heaven in a fit of fire.

But there you stand, sky's salute
around you, still above me. I drown
again in the marvel of you. You are laughing
at my awkwardness on the ledge, an unshod god
from the frieze caught with his paws
in the air, fir for flying, yes, but not as well
as you. I crab back down to where men dwell,
abandoning you to the altitude of birds.
Blinded by you, I tell everyone
who will listen that there, up on the bluff
of the temple, I heard an angel fall.

Boys in White Togas

The fleece of the lamb
from which their togas are woven is no more soft
    than the pubescence on their own
underbellies. Always velvet at that age,
  at that age always blond, it is hardly seen
    unless rubbed up by sunlight
or with droplets of spray from the shower caught
    in it, much as the spider's web
reveals itself at dawn spangled through with dew.
    The boys themselves call it "peach fuzz",
though they have never tasted the fruit
beneath the fuzz. Some of them have a purple band
  on their togas, won not from murex
but from Rit, to indicate that they are meant
  to be nobility. One boy has a bruise

at least on his neck,
almost as purple as the band on his toga. He tried
    to hide it when the boys dressed.
He is not the most beautiful boy, but his eyes engage
  everyone else's. The piping starts,
    in Latin, a flock of larks
interspersed with grackles when the voices crack.
    They turn, process. Their heights ebb
toward the front, the first boys bearing fasces. If men of Rome
    were not as tall as we thought,
  these boys might all be Romans. As they go,
the one boy will not glance my way. He has scanned
  the room and blushes, seeing the mural
of the twins at suck forever in cement,
  or thinking of my mouth against his throat.

Tea Fields Are in Bloom

This is a breathy night. The stream grinds
so hard it winds the steam away from me.
In the low dark, tea blossoms from their green bells
ring out white and clear above the clatter of leaves.
        I have seen how the forked trains
become one here at the end of the platform,
their going and coming pulling them at great lengths
toward their terminals. You would have liked these trains;
you would have liked their glide, their chatter and glare
        streaking the mountains. Sometimes I wake
to their wail and reach for you and their light peals

in the empty room in slashes. The moon
        chokes the stream below with brilliance. The track
here, softened by the moon, flows two with the stream.
When I pass beneath the bridge, if I walk slow,
        the last return tonight will pass
my head in thunder, its wheels grating out sun
on the rails. If you were here, we would stop short
at a neighbor's field and pick in sprig those stars
that are glittering the bushes. Be here. I stop,
        but I do not pick. I want nothing
here and hurry uphill to my house, a house, not home.

The President's Helicopter Passes Over our Land

Sumacs lie strewn about me,
felled by hurricane, their Egyptian cottons rinsed
already of all their starch. My puny arms bulge
to hero size; Samson with jawbone
of an ass still in his hand,
I tower over all my weedy enemies.
There, where the doe lay down with the fawn
among the tree ferns, I lay me down.
The field is salt hay beneath me; the air is rank
with sumac spunk and I soon drift off
into a poppy world. Suddenly, a whir stirs
the sun and I surface from my dream
of bamboo rooms, their heat stirred by ceiling fans.

The sweet young punk vanishes
from my arms. I look up and see a dragonfly
at twelve o'clock, nose due west toward the air force base.
If the superman inside that plane
looks down, he will see a white man,
turned to an Asian brown by a summer at home,
stark still in the thicket. He would not guess
that I, too, am one of his homeless ones.
I might be a sniper lying in wait, my aim
straight for the underbelly; how easily
the junk would crash into our woods. He is safe,
for now, in his inviolate office.
The mighty blades do not even riffle our grass.

The Sky Is Falling

for May Sarton

We have had two wines,
            one white, one red, and our veins
         are buzzing with both. Soon summer ends
and the sun weaves its last full gold through our field,
             drawing from its grass
sunbursts starrier and yellower than itself.
Soon I will have to leave. We feel the sun daze
         through the window, the three of us, but our thoughts
         suddenly scud over in three ways.
After lunch, we drive her home. She waves us in,
in toward the garden. Blue is drifting in its nets,

clouds and clouds of it,
         Aster frikarti. So frail
        is she that the air works against her,
lapping one wing of her coat as she wades green,
          backlit by the sky,
reaching out to catch some blue for us from that flag
full of blue. September in one of its moods
         roughs up. The restless ones are on its winds,
         torn toward their south. We watch them stretch on,
trailing their legs and calling. She stands with the one
I love and the sky, the sky is in their hands.

Shadblow Spring

The blooms are bitter, white as my heart
    after a winter with you.
The wind blows off the river, bringing up its frost
    onto our land. The spiky stars shake
    on their stems. I feel the gust of cold
and I shake with them, shake not so much by bone
as from the core in me, thinking as I do
    how close we have stood, all through snow time,
    at the brunt of each other. You see rave
    and rage in me. It is there,
true, love and hate, love and hate, but it is not
    anger, really, it is the dying back
of my hold on you, the drying at the root

    until I break at a touch. The wind
    drops, though, and the fog comes up
along the river and the new grass is lost
    in it. It is spring, and the skies take
    sudden turns. The shadblow's spurs unfold
and I smell the hidden sweetness. My thoughts of you hone
back to their old sharpness. Year by year the space
    around me grows and I blaze alone.
    No one comes within reach of that cave
    of mine. Only you are here,
too deeply rooted in my love to make a run
    from me, too stunted by me to bloom,
the leaves you do put out forever green with rain.

Smoking Golden Bat

Right in my line of sight is Thin Man,
firenze in blue on his T-shirt. I am not
   watching him; I am warding off
   the man across the table from me.
We are seated on the *zashiki*, a platform
leafed with *tatami*, he in symposium pose,
   right leg raised, right wrist hooked on the knee,
smoke snarling from the end of that blunt cigarette
crouched between two fingers. His face has drained clay-white,
   shading from annoyance to anger. I choke
back my words "to turn away wrath" but he growls,
"Don't raise your voice," and stubs the glow in his hand
   at me. The saké flows and he reels

   as he bends to sip it;
but there is more to his meanness than this drink.
   I catch Thin Man's look flick to one side,
   the only one here to hear us, as I think back
to last week, this man's lips brazened by red wine
prolonging on my mouth a series of moves
   through sixteen bars into one vast kiss.
I recall, when we saw the herms on display,
how surprised we were that Jomon Man so adored
   the phallus (at least in the artist's view),
as I do, as Hindus adore Shiva's shaft,
the lingam, bowing before it, and each night
   I have dreamed him straddling me, the lift

in his long smooth stone thrusting its way
up my belly between the muscles of my chest.
    I toy with the tiny pack, two spread bats,
    head to head, gilt on brown, Sweet & Mild
it says. These bats suck fruit. In China the bat
is a symbol of longevity; my tease,
    though, is lost on him. His life may short
out rather in a fit than by these few sweet smokes.
I know you are afraid that left alone here
    in this village with him, I may take him
upon myself, on opponent's turf a new king.
But we are both poets (or both of us claim
    to be). We will never get along.

A Time to Plant Roses

We are rooted to the land
by heart. Our hold, though, is tenuous. Moss keeps
to its rock through a network of threads
so strict that even though its froth of stars browns out
with thirst, the whole mass goes back to plush
again at the first stroke of wet.
Living in foreign cities, we think
ourselves a crown of such cat's-eye green
when we think of this place, for you a farm, for me
estate, upright one day, I hope, with long parades
in hawthorn white. I was reminded this spring
of our persistence when I found runs
from last year's bamboo grass, yards from where it was then.

The hard Maine winter did not kill
this stranger. Now the cold weeps seaward through our field
beneath a march of trumpet yellow; the same
yellow is the witchery on the forsythia's twigs,
bales of it. Now is the time to plant
roses. These are husky ones, proud
of their age, roses known by Latin and French:
Rosa gallica, L'Imperatrice Josephine,
Tour de Malakoff. Their claws dig into the spice
of our soil, establishing there a base
for their fragrant statuary. This is our best bid
yet for permanence, and as we set them
we work into the land with each rose, hands down.

Goldfinches in the Field

Late afternoon, and as I look up
from a nest I am digging for yet one more
　　flock of irises, I see cloth-of-gold
　　　　settled in the goldenrod,
dozens of light-embodied birds, their yellow gold
　　heightening the medieval red-gold
on the flower plumes. The sun skews through both these golds,
　　shadowing in waves to the east of each crest.
Wanting to catch the Midas touch, I guess, I wade
in after them, through green gone purple; I slink,
　　more wildcat than man, sinking to the chest
　　　　in it. The birds are two yards
　　away, so close I see the black bars crossed

on their wings, black frost above their eyes.
They pinch on the stems of things, bustling their beaks
　　through the ruffle and the razzle. I let
　　　　the thistles, curse on all my lawn,
go to seed for them, but here they are made bold
　　by some other sweetness; as I close in
to see, they keep one rein-length ahead of me,
　　leading me where I let them. They blurt
through the purple-green shade from aster to joe-pye weed,
blue-purple floss to red-purple bolls. I brink
　　on the woods. The goldfinches bob off
　　　　through strands of the sun and I catch
　　here by magic in the weaver's art.

In the Connecticut Suite

All the summers of our lives we haved lived life
together, so much so that when the trees leaf out
their green means you. The leaves on their branches count
my days with you. Not childhood, of course, that prom
toward life, but even before we met some shade
from you was in my weave, some tone of your voice
was in every air I heard. In this great town
where I paid out much of my youth, the snow sheds
fold by fold on every street. The sounds at night
are mulled in its thickets. Passers-by go hush
through furs of it. We gaze down at a satin place

as we dress for New Year's Eve, you in back and white,
I in black and white. This is a photograph
of a younger night, a more colorful night.
We are both just as slim but our skin has flagged
a little, our eyes have lost a few bright coals
from their glow. We drink champagne from glasses chilled
to frost point. You tie my tie, I tie your tie.
We are bandboxed, ready to step out into the dance.
At the door I stop to look at a print, *Deer Hunt*,
stag bleeding onto the snow. I take your hand,
thinking how as the snow melts that blood goes cold.

Night without Its Quicksilver

Just before the brink of sleep,
I roll left to touch a long-familiar warmth
    and wake with a clutch of sheet in my fist.
    My eyes will not force shut; an absence,
its base in places the imprint of his form
    still in the mattress, eats at my sight
with streetlight filtered through a paper window:
    here there always was a silhouette.
    Within a week, the space will be possessed
and I will press the matrix of my body
    against smooth young skin. The test

    will not work. My hand feels
a difference. All those nights, those empty nights, a world
    to go before I lie with him there,
    no one can own that merest fragment
of my past with him. As I smolder and stare
    at the negative space next to me,
I reach out and see my universe disappear.
    Death is less equivocal. Friends speak
    of a growing numbness and how desire
can conquer loneliness with a newcomer
    for me. That is what I fear.

Foxes in the Field

Just as we are locking up at night
we hear barking from the north side, sharp on sharp.
No, it is not a dog. Sharper and shorter and shocked.
    Out over the field I edge, flashed light
    picking up glints from leaves, then cat's-eyes
gleaming out between saplings. If it is mad,
I am rash to go farther, so I hang back,
    prodding. Across the street, Claire as ghost
in white at her window sees vixen with kit
raving up and down. Next morning, as I kneel
    weeding the iris bed, three rush past

    the blackberry patch, the two kits fast
and frisking. Fixed in place, I sit back and watch,
downwind, no risk of being seen, they are too lost
    in romping. Gray foxes, grizzly-backed,
    with rust-red ears and neck, black-tipped tail,
they are hard to see at night and hardly seen
in daylight. They are making a gift of themselves here
    in our garden, as though to have me build
a shrine with two stone fox-gods in front of it.
And in this fallow weather, I think of you
    where foxes live and my heart is healed.

On the Heights of Machu Picchu

Fold by fold the mists sink
   down the mountains, their fleece rubbing off
on fire scars and lightningbreak in rock face. We sit
     up in the sun, its fine gold
flooding the green around us, that green
starred with wild dahlias. Across from us the town
   soars with its terraces rank by rank
     in ever closer overtones,
  but though we float here in this thin sea
at the top of the world, the air so fair one gaze
     goes right to the vanishing point,
the upmost ranks are higher than our eyes' gaze can reach.
This town has long been dead, but it is not dead;
  it is not lived in but now, as cliffs freeze

lightfall into two parts,
   purple and gold, it is lived all over its stones
by a glow the laws of light will not allow,
    and though our bodies are rich
  with our own blood, it is not the hum
in our ears we hear singing along the slopes.
  Today we climbed, climbed, up onto the shelves
    that the llamas graze, their hooves
  tapering down to a sureness our hands
can only grope for; there, as we watched hawks dive
    straight down, never has my heart
been so high and I touched you to steady you
as I touch you now, knowing that all my life
  with you is the only life I have.

Also published by Leviathan

Jackie Wills

Party

ISBN 1-903563-03-8 (cased)

1-903563-04-6 (paperback)

Kit Wright

Hoping It Might Be So

ISBN 1-903563-00-3 (cased)

1-903563-01-1 (paperback)